Walt Disney's

PETER PAN
in Tinker Bell and the
Pirates

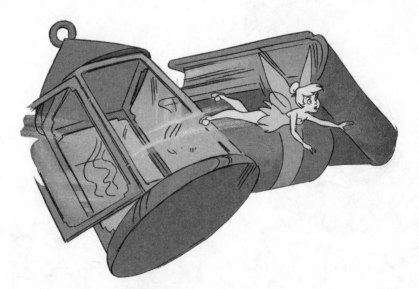

Based on Walt Disney's PETER PAN

A GOLDEN BOOK • NEW YORK
Western Publishing Company, Inc., Racine, Wisconsin 53404

Once there was a magical place called Never Land. Tinker Bell the pixie lived there. So did Peter Pan and his crew of Lost Boys.

Tinker Bell was Peter's special friend. Whenever Peter flew high above the forest, Tink flew with him. Sometimes she sprinkled the boys with pixie dust, and they flew too.

Tink was a busy, happy little sprite.

But then, one day, everything changed.

Peter Pan brought his friend Wendy and her brothers Michael and John to Never Land.

Suddenly it seemed that Peter had no time for Tinker Bell. He went flying with Wendy instead.

The Lost Boys went tiger-hunting with John and Michael, and they didn't ask Tink to come along.

Tink was hurt and jealous. Didn't Peter love her anymore?

The pirate Smee found her one day when she was sitting alone, thinking angry thoughts, and he chuckled with glee.

"Won't Captain Hook be glad to talk with this little pixie!" he said to himself, and he scooped Tink up in his cap and carried her off to the pirate ship that was anchored in the cove.

Captain Hook grinned a sly grin when he saw Tink. "The pixie can help us get rid of our enemy, Peter Pan!" Hook whispered to Smee.

Then Hook turned to Tink. "Ah, Miss Bell," he said, "I hear that Wendy has come between you and Peter Pan. You mustn't feel bad. In the morning we sail away from Never Land. If you wish, we'll kidnap Wendy and take her with us."

"Kidnap Wendy?" Smee looked puzzled. "But how? Wendy's always with Peter Pan, and we've never been able to find his hideout."

Tinker Bell said nothing. Tink never spoke. Instead she made a jingling noise. Then she flew to the captain's map of Never Land and pointed to Hangman's Tree.

It was as if she were saying, "Here's Peter's hideout!"

"Thank you, my dear," said the wily Captain Hook.
"You've been most helpful."

   With that he shut Tink up in one of the ship's lanterns.
Then he and his band of villains headed for Hangman's
Tree.

The pirates waited outside Peter Pan's hideout.

John was the first to see them, but before he could shout a warning, the pirates seized him.

They snatched Wendy too, together with all of the Lost Boys.

Smee was disappointed. "We didn't get Peter Pan," he said. "Where could he be?"

"Don't worry about Pan," said Captain Hook. He showed Smee a box that was tied with a ribbon. It had a note on it that read,

"To Peter, with love from Wendy.
Do not open till six o'clock."

"This will take care of Pan," said Captain Hook. He put the box in Peter's hideout.

The pirates hurried back to the ship with their captives.

"Now then," said Hook, "you all have a choice. Join my pirate crew—or walk the plank."

"Be a pirate?" said Wendy. "Never!"

"We won't walk the plank, either," declared Michael. "Peter Pan will save us!"

"Oh no, he won't," said Hook with a nasty chuckle. "We left a present for Pan. Any second now he'll open it, and be blasted out of Never Land. You'll never see Peter Pan again!"

"Oh, no!" cried Wendy. "A bomb!"

Tink heard! She heard everything!

For a second she was too frightened to move. Then she began to throw herself against the glass walls of the lantern. She rocked back and forth until at last the lantern toppled over.

The door fell open, and Tink was free.

Up she flew, away from the pirate ship and on to Hangman's Tree.

It was two seconds to six when she darted into Peter's hideout.

Peter was just opening his present.

Tink flew at him and pushed the box away.

BOOM! The bomb went off.

For a moment the hideout was thick with black smoke.
Then the smoke cleared. Peter Pan was safe.

But what about Tinker Bell?

Tink lay crumpled in a heap. Her eyes were closed. She
was so still. Was she breathing?

Peter cradled the pixie in his hands. "Tink, speak to me! Please, Tink. You mean more to me than anything in the world."

Tinker Bell heard, and her heart gave a little thump. She made a tiny jingling sound.

"That's it, Tink!" cried Peter Pan.

The jingling grew louder. It was joyful now. Tink knew that Peter loved her. He always had!

Aboard the pirate ship, Hook and his crew were getting ready to make their prisoners walk the plank.

"You first!" said Hook to Wendy.

Little Michael began to cry. "Good-bye, Wendy," he called.

Wendy, we love you!" said her brother John.

Wendy smiled at them. Bravely, she stepped onto the plank and walked out over the water. Then she dropped from sight.

Hook waited to hear Wendy splash into the water. But there was no splash. Instead, a shout came from high in the rigging.

"Hook, you're a codfish!"

It was Peter Pan! Wendy was with him, safe and smiling. He had snatched her up before she hit the water.

"Pan!" cried Hook. "You rascal! I'll get you this time!"

Hook charged at Peter, waving his sword. Peter only laughed. He flew down and darted at Hook. His blade flashed.

Swish! He cut the feather off Hook's hat.

Peter cut the ropes that bound the prisoners.
Seconds later they were all battling the pirates. The
boys threw sticks and stones. John swung his umbrella.
Michael tucked a cannonball into his Teddy bear and
began swinging it.

Soon the pirates were scrambling off the ship, fighting to get into a lifeboat.

Across the deck went Peter Pan and Captain Hook, dueling furiously. Suddenly Hook tripped and stumbled over the side of the ship!

He fell right into the sea, where an eager crocodile waited.

Captain Hook knew that crocodile. It was the croc that had eaten Hook's hand long ago. It had been following Hook ever since, hoping to get the rest of him.

"Smee! Help!" Hook screamed.

Hook swam off, with the croc snapping at his heels. The pirates rowed after the croc, and none of them were ever seen in Never Land again.

Peter Pan took command of the ship, and the Lost Boys cheered.

Wendy cheered, too. "You've won, Peter!" she cried.

Tinker Bell flew over to Peter. She jingled merrily, as if to say, "Peter Pan always wins, didn't you know that?"

Tink was very happy. Wendy and the boys were safe. And she herself would never be jealous again. For she knew that Peter Pan loved her more than anyone else in the world!